MOVING OUT

with the Christian faith

MOVING OUT
with the Christian faith

Peter Jeffery

The challenge of Acts for today's church

EVANGELICAL PRESS

EVANGELICAL PRESS
Faverdale North, Darlington, DL3 0PH, England

e-mail: sales@evangelicalpress.org

Evangelical Press USA
P. O. Box 825, Webster, New York 14580, USA

e-mail: usa.sales@evangelicalpress.org

web: http://www.evangelicalpress.org

First published 2006

British Library Cataloguing in Publication Data available

ISBN-13 978-0-85234-609-9 ISBN 0-85234-609-3

Printed and bound in Great Britain by Biddles Ltd,
King's Lynn, Norfolk

CONTENTS

INTRODUCTION

The Acts of the Apostles is a title that is not part of the original writing and was added about the middle of the second century. The book makes no pretence to record the ministry of all the apostles, only two, Peter and Paul. A more appropriate title would be The Acts of Jesus Christ (1:1) or The Acts of the Holy Spirit. The book covers a period of about 30 years and is a thrilling account of the birth and growth of the church. Blessings and problems go hand in hand, and both are used by the Holy Spirit to accomplish God's purposes.

Acts was written by Luke, probably about A.D. 65. The book is of great importance in the historical framework of Scripture because it is a bridge between the Gospels and Paul's writings. Both his and the other epistles are much more meaningful when they are read in the context of Acts. In Acts we see the founding of the various churches and in the epistles we see the life and problems they face. The book pulsates with life as the Holy Spirit gives power to the preaching, promotes love for the brethren, and guides and instructs in all areas of church life. This is why it is so vital a book today. The church in Acts was utterly dependent upon God. It sought prayerfully the will of God and inevitably it was the Lord who added to the church such as should be saved. The determination to obey Jesus and spread the gospel worldwide is a lesson for us.

All this does not mean that the church in Acts was free from faults and quarrels. There were jealousies (Acts 6) and leaders had differences of opinion that became very sharp and contentious (Acts 15). But these were not allowed to dominate the scene or cloud the main issue and mar the work. The church in Acts was not perfect but it was powerful. It was not without its faults but it was faithful.

Perhaps a word of caution needs to be sounded concerning some of the actions of the young churches in Acts. We are to take our pattern for the Christian life from the teaching of Scripture, not from all the actions of the characters recorded in Scripture. For instance, the selling of possessions in Acts 2:44,45 and 4:32 was carried out with the highest motives, but is that to be the pattern of how we are to conduct our lives today? The New Testament has much to say about the giving of money to maintain the church and to help those less fortunate than ourselves, but we are never commanded to sell all our possessions and share everything. The selflessness behind the action is to be copied by us because it is commanded throughout Scripture, but the particular actions are not obligatory, because they are not commanded.

It is difficult for us today to fully understand the church in Acts with its vibrant life and uncompromising faith. It is all so different to most churches today, but this is how God intends that his church should be. The pattern is there for us and we should make every effort to copy it. Here is a church moving out with the gospel, in obedience to the Lord's command. It was no easy task. The world did not welcome the Lord's people and all manner of difficulties were put in their way; but they were faithful to the command.

SUMMARY

As we have seen, Acts is a history of the planting and extension of the church, but how was this achieved? As you read Acts, the answer becomes very clear. The planting and extension was done by the preaching of the Word of God in the power of the Holy Spirit. So the book can be seen basically as the record of the ministry of the two preachers who were the apostles to the Jews and Gentiles, Peter in the first twelve chapters and Paul in the remaining chapters. Obviously there is some overlapping but it is the preaching of these two men that dominates Acts. As well as these two great men, the whole church is involved in spreading the gospel (Acts 8:4).

The book opens with the Christians still not clear as to the worldwide purpose and extent of the gospel. Just before the ascension they ask Jesus, 'Lord, are you at this time going to restore the kingdom to Israel?' (1:6). These men were Jews and they still kept to the traditional belief that it was the Jewish people exclusively who would receive God's blessing. This misconception was to surface on many occasions in the early church and cause serious problems (see Acts 10:9-23; 11:19f; 15:1). The Lord's answer to the question was that when the power of the Holy Spirit came to them, their witness was not to be confined to Jerusalem but was to go to the ends of the earth.

Acts 2 records the coming of this Holy Spirit power at Pentecost. The most important fact of Pentecost is not the sound of the violent wind or the tongues of fire, or even the Christians speaking in other tongues, but that the people heard the wonders of God. Because this was declared in the power of the Holy Spirit, three thousand were brought to a saving knowledge of the Lord Jesus. This continued to be the main feature of Acts. Miracles took place which astounded the people, but it was preaching in the power of the Spirit that caused them to cry out, 'What shall we do?' The answer was always, 'Repent and believe' (see Acts 2:38; 3:19; 26:20).

The emerging church experienced a great sense of oneness (2:42-47; 4:32-37). There was love, fellowship and growth but there were also problems. Some of these were external, such as the opposition of the Sadducees in chapter 4, but the more serious problems were internal, as we see recorded in chapters 5:1-10 and 6:1-7.

Ananias and Sapphira were members of the church. That meant that they had professed faith in Christ, had been baptized, and the church recognized them as true believers. Yet those two conspired together to lie to the church, which was in effect nothing less than lying to the Holy Spirit (5:3).

This incident could have devastated the young church and it certainly served as an example of the seriousness of sin (5:11). Whether Ananias and Sapphira were ever truly converted will always be open to doubt, but the problem that arose in Acts 6 was among men and women of whom there is no doubt that they were true believers. This was potentially more dangerous than the Ananias and Sapphira incident because it could have split the church on ethnic lines. But with great wisdom the apostles dealt quickly and fairly with this powder-keg, and the result was that the Word of God spread (6:7).

The inevitable persecution against the church continued and, in chapter 7, Stephen became the first Christian martyr. To lose a man of his outstanding qualities in such a way could have devastated the church. But God is good, and from the depths of chapter 7 we are taken to the soaring heights of remarkable blessing in chapter 8. Then the most amazing thing of all happens in chapter 9 and Saul of Tarsus, the great enemy of the gospel, is converted. This was so unexpected that at first the Christians in Jerusalem did not believe that he was now one of them (9:26). The strength of Paul's opposition to Christianity is hinted at in verse 31. With that opposition now ceased, the church enjoyed a time of peace.

Meanwhile, Peter continued his ministry. Chapters 10 and 11 were of vital importance for the fulfilling of Christ's command in 1:8 that the gospel was to be preached to the ends of the earth. Up to this point there had been very little effort made to preach to Gentiles, so God once more takes the initiative. Firstly, he gives Peter the vision of the sheet from heaven (10:9-16). The purpose of this was to overcome Peter's Jewish prejudice against preaching to the Roman centurion, Cornelius. Peter then preaches to him and Cornelius is saved. A new understanding begins to dawn upon Peter (10:34-36) but the other apostles still have their Jewish anti-Gentile prejudice and Peter has to convince them otherwise (11:1-17). They are convinced and the true breadth of God's grace is for the first time recognized: 'God has granted even the Gentiles repentance unto life' (11:18).

This was a great breakthrough but in spite of 11:18, we read in the next verse that they were still preaching only to Jews. The real breakthrough comes at Antioch when the gospel is preached to the Greeks and a great number of these Gentiles believe. Antioch then becomes the church from which the first two missionaries are sent out (13:1-3).

Paul's first missionary journey is recorded in chapters 13 and 14. On the journey there was opposition (13:8) and disappointment (13:13; see also 15:37,38) but there was also great blessing, and Paul and Barnabas gave a thrilling report to the church at Antioch on their return.

This first venture with the gospel into Asia Minor raised, for some, a very serious problem and this is dealt with at the Council of Jerusalem as recorded in chapter 15. The issue is stated very clearly in verse 1. Would the Gentiles have to become Jews if they were to become Christians? The Judaizers said 'yes'. Paul and Barnabas said 'no'. The dispute was settled at Jerusalem, where Paul and the Judaizers argued their respective cases before the apostles.

Chapters 15:36 – 21:16 describe the second and third missionary journeys as the gospel is taken further afield still, and eventually into Europe for the first time. This covers a period of about ten years. When the apostle returns to Jerusalem, he is warmly received by the Christians there, but he is soon in trouble with the Jews (21:27-36). He is arrested and such is the hatred of the Jews that he has to be moved from Jerusalem to Caesarea for his own safety. Two years are spent in prison at Caesarea (chapters 24 to 26) until Paul is dispatched to Rome to plead his case before Caesar.

The two years' imprisonment were not wasted by Paul. He took every opportunity to preach the gospel and held nothing back as he preached righteousness, self-control and judgement to the notoriously wicked Felix. The man trembled before the power of the Word of God, but he remained unsaved (24:25-26). His successor, Festus, dismissed the gospel as insanity (26:24) but King Agrippa was not left untouched. His words in 26:28 have been variously translated and interpreted to mean a trivial jest, bitter sarcasm, a burst of anger or sincere conviction. From the context, in which Paul is convinced that Agrippa believes the Scriptures (v. 27), it would seem that the Authorized Version, 'Almost thou persuadest me to be a Christian', depicting sincere conviction, is the best interpretation.

The journey to Rome (chapters 27 and 28) is dramatic and perilous. The storm, the shipwreck and the incident with the snake on Malta all demonstrate what a remarkable man Paul was, and that God's hand was undoubtedly upon him. He had only been in Rome for three days when he started to try and win the Roman Jews to Christ. The book ends abruptly with Paul boldly preaching and teaching about the Lord Jesus Christ.

1.

MOVING OUT

Acts 1:1-11

One of the most frustrating things for a Christian is the loose way the word Christian is used by most people today. All sorts of people are said to be Christian even though their beliefs and lifestyle are so remote from the teachings of the New Testament. Bishops who do not believe in either the virgin birth or the resurrection abound. Prominent people, who in life seemed to deny everything Christianity stands for, die and are buried as if they were great saints. So what is Christianity? What is a Christian?

The safest answer must be that a Christian is a follower of Christ. But even such a basic answer raises problems. Which Jesus Christ is he following? Is he the Jesus of modern thought who was not born of a virgin, did no miracles and never arose from the dead? Or is it the Jesus Christ of the New Testament?

Francis Schaeffer voiced the concern of many when he wrote:

I have come to the point where, when I hear the word 'Jesus' which means so much to me because of the Person of the historic Jesus and his work — I listen carefully

> *because I have with sorrow become more afraid about the word 'Jesus' than almost any other word in the modern world. The word is used as a contentless banner, and our generation is invited to follow it. But there is no rational scriptural content by which to test it, and thus the word is being used to teach the very opposite things from those taught by Jesus. We have come to this fearsome place where the word 'Jesus' has become the enemy of the Person Jesus, and the enemy of what Jesus taught.*

Luke wrote his Gospel and the Acts to show us the real Jesus: 'Many have undertaken to draw up an account of the things that have been fulfilled among us, just as they were handed down to us by those who from the first were eyewitnesses and servants of the word. Therefore, since I myself have carefully investigated everything from the beginning, it seemed good also to me to write an orderly account for you, most excellent Theophilus, so that you may know the certainty of the things you have been taught' (Luke 1:1-4).

The book of Acts is also written to Theophilus who needed to 'know the certainty of the things you have been taught'. This is something every Christian needs to know, particularly young believers. Your whole life is before you, so is the Christian faith worth building the next forty or fifty years on? Is it true? Can it be relied on? You would be a fool to build your life upon a myth, so you need to know.

Luke was a man who 'carefully investigated' everything he had heard about Jesus Christ. He spoke to eyewitnesses and obtained from them the facts 'about all that Jesus began to do and to teach'. So if you want to know the truth about Christianity there can be no better person to ask than Luke. In his Gospel he takes us right up to the ascension of Jesus to heaven. Now in Acts, which is just as much about Jesus as is the Gospel of Luke, he continues the story of Jesus.

Acts relates the acts of Jesus through the Holy Spirit in the lives of his people. There is no human explanation of what is to follow in this book apart from the power of the living Jesus at work. The Christian faith is not based upon a dead martyr but upon a living Saviour who died and then rose from the dead. This may seem incredible to some but Luke says that Jesus 'gave many convincing proofs that he was alive'. And what can be more convincing than that over a period of forty days after his resurrection he appeared to his people to rebuke, encourage and instruct them?

Luke singles out just one of these appearances in verses 4-5. This is the explanation of the amazing events that are to follow. Jesus baptized his apostles with the Holy Spirit and this gave them the power to do all that Christ wanted them to do. The 'few days' of verse 5 refers to Pentecost which was ten days after the ascension. In the account of Pentecost in Acts 2 we are not told they were *baptized* with the Spirit, but *filled* with the Holy Spirit. In fact the phrase 'baptized with the Holy Spirit' is not used again in Acts, whereas on several occasions we are told of Christians being 'filled' with the Spirit. The one exception is verse 16 in chapter 11, which refers back to this verse in chapter 1:5. The reasonable deduction from this is that being baptized with the Spirit and being filled with the Spirit refer to the same thing.

Witnesses

If we are to know power to witness we need to be filled with the Holy Spirit. Witness is not a matter of technique but of the power of Christ working in us and through us.

Many Christians are timid about witnessing. To counter this a great many different methods and schemes of personal evangelism have been devised. This is all done with the best of intentions, but it does not provide the answer to the problem. It makes witnessing too mechanical and artificial, so that instead of being a natural overflow, it becomes rather the scraping of the bottom of the barrel.

What verse 8 makes clear is that we will never witness properly for Christ without the enabling power of the Holy Spirit. Witnessing flows out of worship. Too many older Christians tell new converts that the first thing they need to do is to learn how to witness. This is wrong. The prime need of the new convert is to learn to worship. This means a living and real experience of God in everyday life. Witnessing will always be difficult unless the heart of the believer is absorbed in God. Being absorbed in God is the product of being filled with the Spirit of God. The believer who is filled with the Spirit cares only about pleasing God and being obedient to him. His life is controlled by the Holy Spirit, centred in Christ and seeks at all times to honour God. Witness then becomes inevitable.

You must never forget that once you are known as a Christian, everything you do is a witness. It may be a good witness or a bad witness. Your behaviour is every bit as important as your words. People will quite rightly dismiss all you say if they do not see the gospel having an effect upon your life. Witnessing, therefore, is not an occasional happening, but a twenty-four-hour business.

Your life will show where you stand with God, but it is your words, more than anything else, that will show unbelievers where they stand. The gospel *must* be spoken (Romans 10:14). The people in your home, school, factory or office need to hear of God's love and offer of salvation. If you do not tell them, it may well be that no one else will.

You must never confine your witnessing merely to giving a testimony of your own experience of God. This can, of course, be included, but your purpose must be to present people with the gospel. They must be shown that they are sinners (Romans 3:23), under the wrath and judgement of God (Romans 1:18) and already condemned by God (John 3:18). You must tell them that God demands repentance (Acts 3:19; 17:30) so that they can then turn in faith to Christ for salvation (Ephesians 2:4-9; John 1:12).

In your witness, do not be arrogant or aggressive. On the other hand, do not be timid or apologetic. Speak naturally and warmly of the things of God. Do not be over-concerned about proving a point and winning an argument. In all this, it is clear that we need the power of the Holy Spirit.

The Second Coming

The ascension must have been an amazing event to see and the Christians looked on in wonder as Jesus disappeared into the clouds. But the angels had the great encouragement for them that this was not the end of Christ's dealings in this world. He would come again (v. 11).

The promise of the second coming of Christ was no new doctrine. Jesus had referred to it in several parables. So they had heard it before but the present circumstances demanded that they be reminded. It is the same with us. We live in a day when sin is so aggressive and arrogant that it is easy to lose heart. 'Has Christianity any future?' seems to be a fair question. So we too need to be reminded that Christ has not finished with this world. He will return (v. 11).

The second coming of Jesus will be:

- Physical — *this same Jesus* — risen, alive and glorified;
- Visible — he will be seen by all (Matthew 24:30);
- Triumphant — he will come to rule.

All this should be a great encouragement to us (1 Thessalonians 4:18). Yet it should also keep us vigilant because we do not know when Jesus will come (1 Thessalonians 5:6). Throughout the centuries there have been Christians who have been fascinated in trying to work out when the Second Coming will take place, whereas, in fact, we ought to live every day as if the Lord was returning now. This doctrine should encourage sanctification not speculation.

The task facing the early church was immense but they were given the incentive of Acts 1:11 and the promise of the power to accomplish it in verse 8. The same incentive and promise ought to motivate us today.

2.

MOVING OUT

Acts 1:12-26

The disciples had been told by Jesus to wait for the gift of the Holy Spirit (v. 4). Waiting did not mean just sitting around idly, although it is true there is no preaching recorded in Scripture from the time of the resurrection to Pentecost. Preaching required power and this they did not yet have; but it did not stop them from praying (v. 14).

There were only about 120 of them and this in itself could have been disheartening. Small numbers often dishearten us in our churches today. But their confidence was not in each other but in the living Christ and what he had promised them. Numbers can be very misleading. After the three-year ministry of Jesus, a group of 120 did not appear many. Was Jesus therefore a failure? Of course not; 120 was soon to become over 3,000 (2:41) and 2,000 years later the number is still being added to.

We would all like to see our churches packed and it is not true that numbers are irrelevant; but they are not the most important thing. What matters is that we never lose our confidence in Christ and never doubt that eventually every knee will bow before him.

Prayer

With this confidence the young church prayed to God. Verse 14 is a tremendous example to us, 'They all joined together constantly in prayer.' Their prayer was not occasional but constant, almost certainly daily. It has been said that they had a ten-day prayer meeting from the ascension to Pentecost; and every one of the 120 was present. When was the last time you were at your church's prayer meeting?

Private prayer is vital, but so too is the prayer meeting, when the whole church comes together to pray. At the beginning of your Christian life get your priorities sorted out and place your church prayer meeting at the top of your list. It is more important than the young people's fellowship, young wives' group, women's meeting, or even Sunday school. If you are too busy to attend the prayer meeting, then *you are too busy.* Robert Murray M'Cheyne said,

> *No person can be a child of God without living in secret [private] prayer; and no community of Christians can be in a lively condition without unity in prayer.*

The devil hates prayer meetings, and is always seeking to destroy them; and often we play into his evil hands. Some Christians pray for far too long, and the majority do not pray at all. This gives rise to murmuring and criticizing and staying away. It is easy to criticize a prayer meeting, but before you do so, first ask yourself if you contributed anything to help the meeting.

The prayer meeting used to be called the powerhouse of the church. That is perfectly correct. So do not despair if it takes some time to get the fire going in the boiler. Persevere. Go along, not to criticize but to pray. *You* pray. You may be young in the faith, but you have as much right to pray as the oldest saint. Help to make the meeting a source of blessing to the whole church.

The place of Scripture in church life

In verse 15 Peter puts before the church the need to appoint a replacement for Judas Iscariot. His proposal was backed by Scripture (v. 20). So we see that from the beginning the church saw the need to be led by what the Bible says.

If the Bible is not our authority, then something else will be, and in all probability it will be our own human understanding. The choice, then, is between what I think and what God has said. To make our own opinion our authority is really a most flimsy foundation on which to build. In recent years there have been two major shifts in the thinking of evangelicals regarding the Bible. Some no longer wholeheartedly accept the inspiration of Scripture, and that undermines any claim that the Bible exercises real authority in their lives. Others, whilst still accepting an orthodox doctrine of Scripture, in actual fact deny by their lives what they say they believe. These two attitudes have been around for a long time (see 2 Timothy 4:3-4; Titus 1:15-16), but in recent years they have been more pronounced.

If there is no supreme authority, then there can be no absolute standards and everything becomes relative. Nothing is right, nothing is wrong. It just depends upon how each individual sees things. So in the world there are no longer any moral standards, and in the church there are no longer any absolute truths. For instance, it is clear from the New Testament that the church in the first century believed in the reality of hell, but today if you believe this you are considered to be very strange, rather outdated and certainly lacking in love.

Without the Bible we have nothing to say to the world that is any different from the moral, and in some cases immoral, platitudes that come from the lips of men who do not know God. We have no substitute for Scripture. An evangelicalism that proclaims the love of God but at the same time avoids the basic New Testament teaching on sin, guilt and judgement, and the need for repentance, is an evangelicalism that is sending souls to hell. It is impossible to be saved without repentance, and repentance is not possible without conviction of sin. Most importantly, there will be no conviction of sin unless men and women are confronted with it.

Why believe the Bible? Let A. W. Tozer have the last word:

> *Within the circles of evangelical Christianity itself there have arisen in the last few years dangerous and dismaying trends away from true Bible Christianity. A spirit has been introduced which is surely not the Spirit of Christ, methods employed which are wholly carnal, objectives adopted which have not one line of Scripture to support them, a level of conduct accepted which is practically identical with that of the world — and yet scarcely one voice has been raised in opposition. And this in spite of the fact that the Bible-honouring followers of Christ lament*

> *among themselves the dangerous, wobbly course things are taking. So radically is the essential spirit and content of orthodox Christianity changing these days under the vigorous leadership of undiscerning religionists that, if the trend is not stopped, what is called Christianity will soon be something altogether other than the faith of our fathers. We'll have only Bible words left. Bible religion will have perished from wounds received in the house of her friends. The times call for a Spirit-baptized and articulate orthodoxy.*

A new apostle

It has been questioned as to whether the church was right to choose another apostle. Some point out that after Acts 1 we never hear of Matthias, so it is deduced that he was never God's choice. This is a weak argument because we hear very little of most of the apostles apart from Peter and John. It proves nothing.

John MacArthur says,

> *Some have argued that Peter and the apostles were mistaken to choose a replacement for Judas. Paul, they assume, was really the Lord's choice as the twelfth apostle. Since there are only to be twelve thrones in the kingdom (Matt. 19:28), the twelfth must be for the greatest apostle, Paul. Nothing in this passage, however, indicates that this action is wrong. It is inconceivable that the Lord would allow such a crucial error in such a crucial office at the very beginning of His church. Why*

> *would He take pains to provide the apostles with all the proper resources, and then allow them to choose the wrong man? Jesus Christ chose Matthias just as surely as He chose the other eleven.*

How do you choose elders and deacons in your church? Do you cast lots as the early church did? In the Old Testament casting lots was the accepted way of finding God's will. This was not regarded as a lucky dip, but as Proverbs 16:33 says, 'The lot is cast into the lap, but its every decision is from the LORD.' So why don't we use this method today? The answer is that today we have a better way of knowing God's will. Acts 1 is the last time in Scripture the lot is used; the coming of the Holy Spirit to lead and guide the church renders it unnecessary.

3.

MOVING OUT

Acts 2:1-13

Pentecost was the fulfilling of the promise of verse 8 in chapter 1. Here was the power that Jesus said was crucial in order to evangelize the world. The physical phenomena, like wind and fire, are nothing like as significant as the spiritual power that came to all the believers. What happened did not affect only the apostles, but 'all of them were filled with the Holy Spirit' (2:4).

With the power of the Holy Spirit these men and women changed the world. The world misunderstood them (v. 13) but it could not ignore them (vv. 6-12). Today we are facing a world that certainly does not understand Christianity but it has no problem in ignoring it. The world sees nothing in the church to attract it or disturb it, and it will have to be disturbed before it will be attracted. Before they ever heard the gospel the people at Jerusalem saw something in the first Christians that made them take notice.

Witnessing is more than telling people they need to be saved. Sinners need to see Christ in us. Is it not true that many people will not listen to the gospel because they have seen the shallowness and inconsistent lives of Christians? Therefore they will not go near a church. If our living does not attract people to Christ then our words never will.

This brings us back to our supreme need to know the power of the Holy Spirit in our lives. The Acts of the Apostles holds before us the enormous possibility, even in the most difficult times, that when the power of the Spirit comes upon the church anything can happen.

Tongues

At Pentecost Jerusalem was filled with pilgrims from all over the world (vv. 9-12). These were Jews who lived outside of the promised land and had made the journey back for the feast of Pentecost. Their reaction to what was happening to the hundred and twenty Christians was one of amazement because they heard them speak in languages that clearly they did not know. So a man from Parthia heard his language being spoken by fishermen from Galilee. No wonder they asked in astonishment: 'What does this mean?'

They were experiencing the impossible and whilst some could dismiss it casually with the words of verse 13, most knew this was no explanation. Drunken men speak nonsense not 'the wonders of God in our own tongues'.

There can be no doubt that the tongues spoken at Pentecost were foreign languages. It was this strange phenomenon that drew the gathering together. But when the crowd was assembled the speaking in tongues stopped, even though they were speaking the wonders of God, and Peter preached to the people in a language they could all understand. It is this preaching that dominates Acts 2. The reaction of unbelievers to the speaking in tongues was, as Paul said in 1 Corinthians 14:23, one of bewilderment and ridicule. But the reaction of the same unbelievers to Peter preaching in the power of the Holy Spirit was, as Paul again said in 1 Corinthians 14:24-25, one of conviction of sin and repentance.

The promise of Acts 1:8 was that they would receive Holy Spirit power and this is clearly seen in Peter's preaching at Pentecost. The only explanation for the fact that fearful Peter could preach in this way, when only seven weeks before he had denied even knowing Jesus, is the power of the Holy Spirit. The 3,000 were not saved by human oratory but by a power that no man could know unless the Holy Spirit gave it to him.

Power today

Since the Reformation, evangelicals have always believed in the necessity of the outpouring of the Holy Spirit, but most have believed that speaking in tongues, like all the miraculous gifts, finished at the end of the apostolic era. This is what great preachers such as J. C. Ryle, Jonathan Edwards, George Whitefield and Charles Spurgeon believed and taught. But without doubt these men knew an extraordinary amount of the power of the Holy Spirit on their preaching — far more, it could be argued, than all the charismatics of the past fifty years. These men experienced revival.

Whether or not you think these great men were right or wrong in believing that the gifts of the Spirit ceased at the end of the apostles' ministry, you must believe that we need the power of the Spirit in the church today. We desperately need this same power that Peter had at Pentecost, that Edwards had in eighteenth-century America and that Spurgeon had in nineteenth-century England.

4.

MOVING OUT

Acts 2:14-41

The most important thing about Pentecost was not the speaking in tongues but the fact that 3,000 souls were saved (v. 41). The tongues are not unimportant but Pentecost is about the Holy Spirit's work of salvation. The proof of this is that in the rest of Acts tongues are rarely mentioned, but almost every page is taken up with salvation.

Peter quotes the Old Testament prophet Joel (vv. 17-21) to explain what has happened in terms of souls being saved. He then goes on immediately (vv. 22-36) to speak of the death and resurrection of Jesus. This is because it is in Jesus alone that God deals with our sin and provides pardon and forgiveness for the guilty sinner. The whole sermon is fixed firmly in the Old Testament Scriptures. It centres on who Jesus is and what he has done, and concludes with a call for repentance. 3,000 people responded to that message and were saved.

The Bible has but one basic message — the glory of God in our salvation. And the three great events in the ministry of Jesus all proclaim the same message. Each is about salvation and each shows clearly that salvation is completely dependent upon God.

- Christmas — if God did not become man, salvation would be impossible.
- Easter — if Jesus did not die for us, our sins could not be forgiven.
- Pentecost — if the Holy Spirit had not been poured out, we would never see our need of salvation and turn to Christ.

The promise of verse 21 is made possible only because of everything that Jesus did.

The atonement

The doctrine of atonement is the biblical teaching on the 'meaning of the death of the Lord Jesus Christ'. The atonement is God's answer to human sin, and, as such, is the only effective answer to our sinfulness and guilt. It is crucial therefore that we have a full biblical understanding of what it means.

God's way of salvation did *not* start in the New Testament when Jesus came into the world. In the Old Testament God ordained certain events that, though important in the lives of the Israelite people at the time, were even more important as vivid illustrations of what Jesus Christ was going to accomplish when he came into the world.

The Old Testament pictures remind us of two basic facts about the atonement. First, it was planned by God. Peter refers to the death of Jesus as being, 'by God's set purpose and foreknowledge' (Acts 2:23). He later says that Jesus 'was chosen before the creation of the world' to shed his blood for us (1 Peter 1:20). God planned it all to demonstrate his love for us (Romans 5:8).

Secondly, there is nothing hit or miss about our salvation. The death of Jesus was not a tragic mistake but 'God's set purpose'. All the events that led up to Calvary were under God's control. When Pilate said to Jesus that he had power to free him or crucify him, Jesus replied, 'You would have no power over me if it were not given to you from above' (John 19:11). God was in charge at Calvary, not Pilate.

The supreme purpose of the Old Testament is to tell us about Christ and his cross. God even sent two of the great Old Testament leaders, Moses and Elijah, to speak to Jesus about the fulfilment of the prophecies dealing with his death (Luke 9:31).

Essential ingredients

Acts 2 shows us the way God applies the gospel to men and women dead in sin. Here we have all the essential ingredients of salvation: preaching the gospel; the power of the Holy Spirit; men and women convicted of sin; and repentance.

Peter's preaching confronted the people with the fact of their sin (v. 23). They had rejected Jesus who was the Christ of God. They heard the truth about Jesus and were brought face to face with the living Saviour. There can be no salvation without this. The truth convicted them. They did not deny their sin or blame the Romans for the crucifixion. The preaching had the effect of cutting them to the heart. It bit deep into their hearts and minds. Theirs was no superficial, emotional response but one that can only arise when the power of the Holy Spirit falls on the preached word. They were convicted of sin and believed the truth about Jesus. This too is essential to salvation; but it is not enough.

The final essential ingredient is repentance. Repentance has two sides: it is a turning *from* sin and *to* God (Acts 3:19). For true repentance both these elements are crucial. A man can turn from sin without turning to God. He may see the value of changing his lifestyle and decide to refrain from certain bad habits. No doubt this will do him good in many ways, but spiritually it will be useless. On the other hand, a man may turn to God and cry for mercy, but have no intention of leaving his sin. His eyes may be wet with tears and his heart as hard as stone.

True repentance involves seeing sin for what it really is; not just a character defect, but a permanent attitude of rebellion against the love and care and righteous authority of God. It is this new understanding of God and of one's own sin that leads to true repentance. There will also be a great desire to break with the past and to live in future only to please God (Acts 26:20). That is repentance.

Baptism

Baptism is not essential to salvation, but it is necessary for obedience to the commands of Scripture. It is not essential to salvation because it follows salvation. It takes place after a person is saved and is an outward sign of the inward work of grace the Holy Spirit has performed in the soul. It is assumed in verse 41 that if a person accepts the gospel and is saved then he will be baptized.

God's way

Peter took the events of Calvary and presented them to the world in the irresistible almighty power of the Holy Spirit. And at Pentecost, the Holy Spirit, using the preaching of the cross, saved 3,000 souls. That is God's way. It always has been and still is today.

For seven weeks the church had the facts of the cross and the resurrection, but they saw no conversions. Facts alone, however glorious and however well presented, have no converting power. Pentecost set the facts on fire by setting the church on fire. The first result of the fire was that unbelievers heard the wonders of God (v. 10); this led to 3000 being saved (v. 41). There is nothing to compare with the power of the Holy Spirit. Peter, who had trembled before the accusation of a serving girl and denied Jesus, now preaches fearlessly the glorious gospel.

We mourn over the sin of this nation, but what will change it? Only the gospel preached in the power of the Holy Spirit; that is, truth and fire. In 1665 the Great Plague swept through London. Out of the population of 450,000 people, 60,000 died of cholera. Men were powerless to stop this terrible march of death. Then came the Great Fire of London, and the plague fled before the flames. In the same way sin, which seems so permanent and immovable, is banished when the Holy Spirit's fire moves in the human heart.

Does your pastor preach with power? If not, one reason may be that you do not pray that the Lord will give him such power. Preachers need their church to pray for unction on the preaching. Unction is that indefinable power of the Spirit that can take ordinary preaching and make it mighty. Samuel Davies, the American minister, said when he first heard George Whitefield preach that the sermon was ordinary but the unction extraordinary. That is what your pastor needs, so pray that the Lord will give it to him.

5.

MOVING OUT

Acts 2:42-47

God deemed it necessary that the church would be crucial for the spread of Christianity. The church was not the idea of the apostles or the other first Christians — God imposed it upon them. The Lord, even in the Old Testament, was concerned that those who came into a living experience of him should also be in a living experience of each other. Acts presents us with the picture of the developing early church.

A sense of awe and wonder at what God was doing and a spirit of oneness among each other (v. 44) marked the life of the church. There was nothing nominal about this Christianity but it vibrated with passion and life.

The priority was doctrine (v. 42). The apostles' teaching was the basis of all that they did, therefore it was top priority for them. Over the centuries Christians have put doctrine before fellowship. This was because fellowship is more than friendship. It is based on a common experience of the saving grace of God and the apostolic teaching is the infallible explanation of the meaning of this grace.

Sadly, in recent years the order has been reversed and top priority given to fellowship. Indeed doctrine has come to be regarded as something that hinders fellowship whereas in the New Testament doctrine gives substance to fellowship. Out of the doctrine came a deep and lasting fellowship in Christ.

The Holy Spirit's ministry in the Christian is first to deepen his knowledge and experience of God and we see this in the four things mentioned in verse 42: doctrine, fellowship, breaking bread and prayer. The Spirit's ministry does not end with these but he never bypasses them because an untaught Christian is an insecure Christian.

The worship of the church flowed out of its life and doctrine and centred again on the four things of verse 42. This produced a genuine praise for God (v. 47) which led to God blessing their ministry with conversions every day. Conversions were the fruit not of special efforts but of the daily life and witness of the church.

Consistency

There is a difference between life and lively. A church can be lively with plenty of activities going on and still be devoid of true spiritual life. It also has to be said that noise is not life. So what sort of life does God want to see in his church?

From verse 42 we can see a consistency and commitment among the believers that is sadly lacking in many churches today. These were no flash-in-the-pan converts. They were no hot and cold Christians — enthusiastic one week and bored and indifferent the next. They were not pick-our-meeting, pick-our-preacher Christians. Rather, every day (v. 46) they devoted themselves (v. 42) to the life and ministry of the church. Their consistency shone out and it had the broad base of doctrine, fellowship, breaking of bread and prayer.

When the life of a church is based on such a solid foundation it will produce Christians whose appetites are for solid food, not froth and bubbles. A new evangelical church was growing rapidly under a solid biblical ministry and was attracting Christians from other churches. This led to the leaders of these churches accusing the new church of sheep-stealing. The answer of an elder of the new church was: 'We do not steal sheep, we grow grass.' Where spiritual food is offered not in a dull, boring way, but with spiritual life and power, Christians will always be attracted to it.

The church is full of good starters but where are the finishers, the consistent ones? The Christians of Acts 2 were not super-saints but very ordinary believers. They were not perfect but they were consistent. The life they lived was consistent with the doctrine they believed. Their fellowship was consistent. They met every day and this was only possible because of the deep bond of love that existed between them.

We can learn much from this to benefit our churches today. You should not expect your church to be any more spiritual than you are. A simple jingle that every Christian ought to take very seriously goes like this: 'If every member was just like me, what kind of church would my church be?'

Something else to remember is that every church consists of sinners. It is true that they are sinners saved by grace but none the less they are far from perfect. One major cause of problems in local churches is that we forget this. We set too low a standard for ourselves and too high a standard for others. We expect much more from them than we are prepared to give ourselves. None of us is perfect in attitude or behaviour, so let us all exercise a little tolerance. This is not to excuse sin but it will help us to be more loving towards each other.

Do not let the devil use you to disrupt your church. A few simple rules could benefit us all, and they start with recognizing our own weaknesses and taking care not to let the devil use them.

- If you tend to be critical, then just shut up for a while!
- If you tend to be opinionated, then let others speak and try to understand their viewpoint.
- If you tend to be envious — don't feed it.
- If you are quick to take offence, remember it is not because you are sensitive but because you are touchy. You can *give* offence unintentionally but you cannot *take* offence unintentionally.

Contagious

We are told in verse 47 that the church had favour with all the people. This was because the life they lived was entirely different from the secular and religious life of the time. Most religion was a sham and most of secular life was a rat race, but these believers exhibited a beautiful and joyous Christ-centred life. People are looking for this today and such a life can be a powerful tool for evangelism.

We talk of certain diseases being contagious, but the most contagious thing the world has ever seen is a church whose life, message and love reflects the character of Jesus. Such a life is like fire — it spreads quickly and nothing can stand before it.

Cwmbran is the only new town in Wales. In the early years of its development the authorities decided to commission a statue to stand in the shopping centre, depicting a family in the new town, of father, mother and child.

One day the statue appeared in its designated spot, all boarded up, awaiting the official unveiling ceremony. People were naturally curious to see what it looked like. Then the great day came and the statue was unveiled. People gasped with amazement at what they saw. The following comments were actually heard:

'What is it?'

'It looks like three drunken worms.'

'It looks better with the boards up.'

The statue caused a great commotion. TV crews came to see and record. The press interviewed people for their opinion on the statue and everyone had a view to express.

What caused the stir was that the statue was in the style of modern art, and very few people liked or understood it. If it had been a conventional statue, no one would have given it a second look. It was the difference that caused people to sit up and take notice.

The Christians in the Acts of the Apostles caused a stir everywhere they went because they were different. Their lives, actions, ambitions and beliefs were different, and people took note of them. Today we try desperately to make our faith acceptable to people by making our Christianity no different from their lifestyle. So Christians go to the pub after church for a drink; Christians laugh at the world's unsavoury jokes; Christians delight in the world's ungodly music. We are desperately trying to show them that really we are exactly like them.

The result is that the church has no effect upon the world. The world ignores us. Why should it bother if we are no different? But the Bible calls upon us to be different; and this difference can be a very important means of evangelism. How often have you heard a testimony of salvation in which the person says that what first attracted him to Christianity was a friend who 'had something that I did not have'?

6.

MOVING OUT

Acts 3:1-10

In the Gospels we see Christ at work directly. He was physically present so he could touch the sick and speak the word that brought Lazarus out of the grave. However, in Acts Christ is not physically present; he has ascended to heaven. But before he went, he told his apostles that they could do nothing apart from him. So at Pentecost Jesus poured out his Holy Spirit to give the church power to do his work. It is still Christ's work in Acts every bit as much as it is in Matthew, Mark, Luke and John. It is Christ working through his church, through men and women.

It ought to be still the same today but sadly we do not see the blessing that is so evident in Acts. There are several explanations for this but Acts 3 focuses on one very important reason. What sort of Christians does God use and work through? Are we usable in God's service?

There is no doubt that as Christians we can be a hindrance to the work of the gospel. Peter was one such hindrance on a particular occasion and earned the rebuke from Jesus that he was acting as Satan's tool. So what are the characteristics that God wants to see in his people? Characteristics that are not sovereignly given like the gifts of the Spirit or natural abilities, but are our responsibility to cultivate in our lives.

It is so easy to excuse our indolence by saying that it is not God's will to bless us in some way; in other words, to hide behind divine sovereignty. But the New Testament will not allow us to do that. In the New Testament divine sovereignty is a great incentive and encouragement to evangelize, not an excuse to explain away our lack of enthusiasm and lack of blessing.

Four qualities

If God is to bless us there are things he requires to see in us. These things we can see in Peter and John in Acts 3.

1. *They were together,* not just physically but spiritually (v. 1). One of the greatest hindrances to blessing is friction between believers. The devil knows this and is always trying to stir up tension in the church.

2. *They were spiritually hungry* — they were going to pray. Peter and John were men absorbed in Christ. Their priorities were God-ward. At three in the afternoon they were going to pray, not out of a sense of duty but a sense of delight.

3. *They were alert to the needs of those around them and took time to stop for a man in need* (vv. 4-6). Perhaps we see so little blessing because we care so little for men and women without Jesus. It is no good praying for God to speak to them if we won't speak to them.

4. *They were men with a complete and utter reliance upon the Lord Jesus* (v. 6). We have something far better than

silver and gold to give to the world. Do you believe this? Do we believe in the sufficiency of Jesus?

These then were the qualities that God was pleased to use and bless. They ought to be in us and can be cultivated.

Cultivate

These four qualities are not given to us but are to be cultivated by us in our lives. We are to work at them. They are not a matter of ability but of commitment and enthusiasm.

If bitterness and strife are the greatest hindrance to blessing, then spiritual apathy runs them a close second. What is your commitment to Christ like? Do you hunger and thirst after God? God is looking for men and women, young or old, who love him, who want him and whose hearts ache for his smile. Being able to be used by God does not mean we must be perfect and never make mistakes — Peter made plenty. But it does mean that our hearts are not fighting God.

You cultivate this in the same way you cultivate plants in the garden — with care, love and much attention. Weeds grow on their own but beautiful blooms need help.

As a young Christian it is easy to get sidetracked by the attractions of the world. There is nothing wrong with many of these attractions. Sport, for instance, is good but it can be too demanding. It can become to you more important than your prayer life. If it does, you have to make a choice — God or the world. This is how you cultivate usability. Give God the top priority and you will be amazed at what the Lord will do through you.

7.

MOVING OUT

Acts 3:11-26

The healing of the beggar gave Peter the opportunity to speak to the crowd. Dr Martyn Lloyd-Jones said,

> *Some people might say this would have been a wonderful opportunity for Peter to preach about miracles, to offer to heal others... Rather, Peter did not, to use modern language, cash in on what had happened. He did the exact opposite. In effect, he said, 'You are marvelling and looking at us, but I want to explain to you what has happened.'*

The explanation lay with God and particularly 'the name of Jesus' (v. 16). The Jesus whom the people had so viciously rejected (vv. 13-16) was responsible for the miracle that had taken place.

The way Peter confronted the crowd with their rejection of Jesus was uncompromising and left them in no doubt as to the enormity of their sin. Christian preaching does not play to the gallery and encourage people to think that they are all God's children. It always deals clearly with the issue of human sin and guilt. This may not be popular but it is the only effective way of bringing sinners to conviction.

Preaching is not meant to entertain but to confront people with God and how they stand before him.

Even though the sin may be committed in ignorance (v. 17), the demand is still for repentance (v. 19). There is no bypassing repentance if you want your sins wiped out; but this is always preceded by conviction. If they refuse to believe what Peter said about their sin then there could be no repentance. Thankfully many did believe (4:4), and repented and became Christians.

Circumstances

We will probably never be in the exact circumstance that Peter found himself, and we may never see crowds of people come running to us to ask about God. But, nevertheless, there are many occasions when the Lord opens up the way for us to speak to an individual. Our circumstances may be different from Peter but our message needs to be the same.

People today need to be told about Jesus. The ignorance of modern man to the facts about Jesus is almost total. They need to be told who he is, what he did and what he expects of them. This inevitably will involve the question of sin and guilt, but it cannot be avoided. Our business in witnessing is not to make the gospel palatable to sinners but to tell it as it is. They need to see why they have to be saved. Our friends may not like it at first but if the Lord has really opened the way for you to speak to them, he will also be preparing their hearts to hear the truth.

Being bold and gentle are the two things we need in personal witness. Being bold will ensure we do not water down the gospel, and being gentle will guard us from being offensive. It is one thing if the gospel message offends sinners, but we should never offend them by our attitude and actions.

Repent

Peter does not invite his hearers to accept Jesus or to open their hearts to the Saviour but rather he commands them to repent. If we need to learn anything from Acts it must be that we get our terminology right about salvation. Today's common phrases among evangelicals such as, 'Receive Jesus into your heart', or 'Accept Jesus as Saviour', or 'Make your decision', are all right as far as they go but they are not phrases found in the New Testament. It is possible to do these things quite sincerely yet without any awareness of personal sin. But it is impossible to repent unless we are convicted of our sin and guilt and therefore of our desperate need of a Saviour.

This being the case, it is not surprising that all the New Testament preachers, from John the Baptist and Jesus on, called upon their hearers to repent of their sin. It is sad that in much evangelistic preaching of the past fifty years the call to repent has all but disappeared. It has been replaced with other words and concepts that are deemed to make it easier for the sinner to come to Christ. Does this make us wiser than the Holy-Spirit-inspired preachers of the New Testament? Or is it that by omitting repentance we may be making it easier for superficial decisions — but we are making it impossible for true biblical conversions?

8.

MOVING OUT

Acts 4:1-22

In the Christian life courage is not a natural characteristic which every believer has. The Christian may be naturally timid and rather hesitant, or he may be bold and extrovert. The courage demonstrated in the New Testament has nothing to do with what we are temperamentally; it is the product of conviction. The great statement of verse 12, 'Salvation is found in no one else, for there is no other name under heaven given to men by which we must be saved,' reveals the strong conviction these believers had as to the uniqueness and exclusiveness of Jesus. It was this conviction that enabled them to boldly defy the authorities and continue preaching the gospel.

Blessing is followed by attack and when Peter clearly sets before the enemies of the gospel the uniqueness of Jesus (v. 12), the result is that the Christians are forbidden to preach the gospel (v. 18). Peter's answer to this in verses 19-20 is the yardstick by which all believers in every age are to act.

To obey God rather than men can be very costly and through the centuries it has cost many Christians their lives. Polycarp was Bishop of Smyrna. About A.D. 156 he suffered a martyr's death at the age of eighty-six. When he was given the usual opportunity to acknowledge publicly the deity of the Roman emperor and to curse Christ, the old man replied, 'Eighty-six years have I served him, and he has done me no wrong; how then can I blaspheme my King who saved me? … You threaten the fire that burns for an hour, and after a little while is quenched; for you are ignorant of the fire of the judgment to come, and of everlasting punishment… Do as you wish.'

If verse 12 is true, and it is, then to refrain from telling the world about Jesus would be just about the worst thing we could do. We ought to be encouraged by the example of Peter, John and Polycarp to be bold in our witness. The courage of verse 13 was not natural but the result of being with Jesus and the conviction of who Jesus is. Being with Jesus refers not just to physical nearness (these men had not known that for a couple of months) but to an ongoing spiritual nearness.

Ordinary men

You may feel you have no outstanding gifts and are a very ordinary person. This may be true but it can be a help rather than a hindrance to Christian witness. In the work of the gospel, cleverness and head knowledge are not the essential ingredients. We need a closeness to the Lord and a longing to be of use to him. These are the crucial things.

Never minimize your potential for usefulness in the work of the gospel. The Christian church was launched by God using ordinary men like Peter and John, and over the centuries God has continued to use 'nobodies'. Of course, God also uses men and women of remarkable abilities. In the Acts, Paul clearly was a very gifted man and he was used mightily, but so too were the unschooled, ordinary Peter and John.

Charles Spurgeon gave the following description of the man who preached the sermon that led to his conversion:

> *A very thin-looking man, a shoemaker, or tailor, or something of that sort, went up into the pulpit to preach. Now, it is well that preachers should be instructed, but this man was really stupid. He was obliged to stick to his text, for the simple reason that he had little else to say. The text was, 'Look unto me, and be ye saved, all the ends of the earth.' He did not even pronounce the words rightly, but that did not matter.*

That Methodist lay-preacher was clearly unschooled and ordinary but his faithfulness to Christ led to the salvation of one of the most gifted and extraordinary preachers the English language has ever had.

Conviction

The conviction held by Peter and John was to the fact of a risen, glorified Christ and to the truth of what he alone had done. Verse 12 oozes with this conviction — *no one else; no other name; we must be saved.* There is no substitute in Christian work for this sort of conviction. It gives urgency and authority to our message and leaves our hearers with no escape hatch. A preacher must have this conviction and so too must a Sunday school teacher. But it is also vital to the individual believer witnessing to a friend.

The world is full of options and uncertainties. People are always being given an either/or choice. The gospel is not like that. It is confident that Jesus alone can save. It centres everything in Jesus. God gives man no alternative in the matter of salvation. Jesus is the only Saviour offered to us. Such a conviction is regarded by the world today as bigoted and intolerant, but your business is not to pander to the views of unbelievers but to declare boldly the word of the living God.

Yardstick

The gospel has never been popular and never will be. The world opposes it with vigour as Peter and John found out when they were forbidden to preach the good news about Jesus (v. 18). Their response to this has become the yardstick by which all Christians are to respond to such opposition. When the choice is to obey God or men, there is only one clear way for us.

John MacArthur says,

> *It is a clearly biblical principle that believers are to obey their government. Peter himself taught such obedience in 1 Peter 2:13-17 (cf. Rom. 13:1-7). The reaction of Peter and John, however, marks the limits of that obedience. They would gladly obey if they could do so without disobeying their sovereign Lord. But when God's commands conflict*

with those of the government, the government must be disobeyed. The actions of the Hebrew midwives (Exodus 1:15-17) and Daniel (Daniel 6:4-10) further illustrate that obligation.

Although Peter and John refused to obey the Sanhedrin, they nevertheless treated them with respect. They did not argue with them, nor pretend to submit and then go and disobey. Instead, they carefully and respectfully explained that they could not stop speaking. Like Paul, who exclaimed, 'Woe is me if I do not preach the gospel!' (1 Corinthians 9:16), they were compelled to speak.

9.

MOVING OUT

Acts 4:23-37

Christians in fellowship with each other, speaking to each other of the mercies of God and then praising the Lord in prayer, are a dynamic force in this world. Never minimize the power of God to work through ordinary believers when their eyes are on the Lord and their prayers are full of Jesus (vv. 24-30).

The willingness of this group of believers to risk the wrath of the authorities resulted in God giving them a great boldness to preach. The restriction put upon them inspired them to a stronger witness and proclamation of the name of Jesus. Not only that, but it also bound them to each other in even greater unity (v. 32).

Great power and great grace (v. 33) are an irresistible combination. The world has no answer to these twins. As Christians we have tools available to us that are way beyond the imagination of man. Therefore opposition should not dampen our enthusiasm for the gospel. Men will always oppose the gospel and seek to silence it, but God always gives power and grace to those of his people who are willing to obey him.

The enthusiasm and commitment of these believers ought to encourage us all. It is not easy being a Christian today but it was harder in the first century. Barriers, restrictions, opposition and persecution did not stop these folk. The more intense the problems, the more determined they became to remain faithful to the Lord.

God saw this determination and strengthened it (v. 31). The more we give ourselves to God, the more he gives of himself to us. What a God!

Their own

Peter and John were not alone in their confidence in the gospel and so as soon as it was possible they 'went back to their own people and reported' on all that had gone on. Peter and John were the leaders, the figureheads, the preachers, but they needed all the support they could get from their fellow believers. Courage can soon wilt if we are left alone to face our enemies. Christians need each other in the work of the gospel and this is the way God has ordained and planned it.

Your pastor needs your support and encouragement. A letter or phone call of support coming at a difficult moment has strengthened many church leaders to go on in the battle. Don't think that nothing you could say could ever possibly encourage your pastor. When Dr Lloyd-Jones was laid aside with illness from the pulpit of the great Westminster Chapel in London he received many letters of encouragement, but one he valued more than most was written by an eleven-year-old girl. She simply said that she was eagerly awaiting his return to the pulpit because he was the only preacher she could understand.

Also, pastors need to learn to share their problems with the church. There will be some problems which cannot be made public but these are usually to do with personal counselling not the public work of ministry. If the church does not know what the pastor is facing, how can they pray for him?

Prayer meeting

The problem confronting the church in Acts 4 did not need discussion, it needed prayer. It did not need the input of 'brother Ruben' or 'sister Anna' as to what to do. What to do had already been rightly decided. They needed the power of God to carry out what they knew to be right. So without any delay the church held a prayer meeting.

In most evangelical churches today the prayer meeting is very poorly attended, and few young people are present at all. Why is this? Is what was so crucial in the first-century church no longer needed in our day? Have we outgrown the need to cry to God for help? The spiritual health of a church can be measured by the importance it gives to its prayer meeting.

Young people often find prayer meetings difficult because of the very long prayers of some older folk, or, even worse, of the mini-sermons that masquerade as prayers. It is easy for youngsters to opt out of the church prayer meeting but that would be wrong. What you need to do is to go there and pray yourself. Many a prayer meeting has been invigorated when a young voice is lifted up in praise and petition to its God.

The prayer

The prayer opens with the words 'Sovereign Lord'. The Greek word for 'Lord' is not the one usually used in the New Testament. The word used here could probably be translated as 'autocrat'. It means absolute ruler and indicates their confidence in the final sovereignty of God. Later on in the prayer the more usual word for Lord is used, but they start their prayer confident in the Lord who will always triumph even when kings and rulers are against him. He is sovereign. He is in control. Even Herod and Pontius Pilate could only do what the Lord 'had decided beforehand should happen'.

Do you have such a confidence in God? You ought to. The content of the prayer was simply that they should be given power to do the very thing that caused them the problem in the first place — 'speak your word with great boldness'. They were not looking for an easy way out but for grace to remain faithful in very difficult times.

As John MacArthur reminds us:

> *The church had successfully faced its initial trial of opposition. Instead of succumbing to the temptation to compromise the gospel, it became even bolder. The persecution also served to draw the congregation closer together and to their Lord. In what was to become a recurring theme in church history, opposition only made the church grow stronger. As He had with Joseph (Gen. 50:20), God took the evil intentions of men and used them for His own purposes.*

The sharing of possessions in verses 32-37 was not a command for all Christians to follow, but a particular expression of love they had for each other. We are to have the same love and to show it, if not in exactly the same way as these early Christians, certainly with exactly the same enthusiasm and concern for each other.

10.
MOVING OUT

Acts 5:1-16

The devil is clever, and sometimes too clever, as we see in Acts 5. If opposition from the world does not work he will attempt to disrupt the church from within.

Ananias and Sapphira were members of the church but their hearts were not in tune with the other Christians as the sorry episode of their lies reveals. It may be possible to fool men but it is never possible to fool God. Through Peter, the Lord deals severely with this husband and wife. Perhaps the devil thought this would hinder the work of the gospel but God used it to strengthen the church. This in no way justifies their action but it does show that the Lord is in control, not Satan.

The great fear of verse 11 was not terror, but awe, as the Christians saw again the reality of God in their midst. This itself became a launch pad for the remarkable blessing of verses 12-16. The reality of God in the church is something we need to crave for today. God is not a stranger but the lover of our souls. He will not tolerate sin but has great patience and a great capacity for forgiveness. We do not see many souls saved these days and it may be that we have lost sight of God's ability to do amazing things in our midst.

We need to capture again a vision of the greatness of God. Awe and wonder ought to characterize our worship and a sense of expectation should never be far away. What God did, he can still do. This is our hope in times of little blessing.

Two questions

Two questions come out of the story in Acts 5. Were Ananias and Sapphira true Christians, and was the punishment for their sin too severe?

There has always been a difference of opinion among Christians as to whether or not Ananias and Sapphira were true believers. Some point to Simon the Sorcerer in Acts 8 to show that no church, whether in New Testament times or since, can guarantee that every single one of its members at any given time is a true Christian. This is obviously right, but it is interesting to compare the words Peter uses to Ananias and Sapphira with those which he addresses to Simon. To Simon he says, 'Your heart is not right before God,' clearly indicating that this man was not saved (Acts 8:21). There is no such indication in his words to Ananias and his wife. But some would object that no true Christian could have his heart filled by Satan. Peter, from his own experience, would know that this is not true (Matthew 16:21-23).

So was the profession of faith made by Ananias and Sapphira false? Had they deceived the church with their claim to be Christians? If that were the case then their sin of lying to God would not perhaps have been too surprising. In any case, all believers are capable of committing just about any sin. The New Testament nowhere seeks to hide the possibility of true Christians falling into sin and numerous examples are given of the sins of God's people.

Whether they were Christians or not does not affect the crucial lesson this story puts before us. Their death was not the result of Peter putting them under pressure. Dr Lloyd-Jones, preaching on Acts 5, put it like this:

> *This is a judicial action on the part of God... God does something to lay down a great principle. God gives an indication to his own people as to who he is and how he acts.*

Hypocrisy

Fooling the church is not too difficult, but fooling God is impossible. If God does not deal with us today in exactly the same manner as he dealt with Ananias and Sapphira, he still does deal with our hypocrisy. This is a sin that Jesus particularly despised. In the Sermon on the Mount he speaks powerfully against it (Matthew 6:1-6,16-18).

Some writers have likened Ananias' sin to that of Achan in Joshua 7. Achan was responsible for the defeat for God's people. Blessing was withheld from the whole nation because of the sin of this one man. Is the same thing happening today in our churches? Could it be that the hypocrisy of a few is holding back blessing?

We need to realize that as Christians we cannot live for ourselves. Everything we do as believers affects other Christians, and this is particularly true in the local church. Directly or indirectly, we all influence each other for good or evil. God tells us that we are members of the body of Christ. We are part of the church, part of a fellowship.

11.

MOVING OUT

Acts 5:17-42

There are none so blind as those who do not want to see. You could provide all the evidence possible for some people as to the truth of Christianity and they would still not believe. In fact the opposite would be their reaction (v. 17) and their opposition would grow. For the Sadducees even the imprisoning of the apostles served to show that the power of God was working with the Christians. But still they would not believe.

In verses 29-32 Peter sums up the whole situation. The most fundamental question in the relationship between God and man is how we regard Jesus. Confronted with Jesus, the world killed him (v. 30). At Calvary the Jews thought they had seen the last of Jesus. But God raised him from the dead so that now we can see him not as a dead martyr but as the risen Prince and Saviour (v. 31).

The Christian sees Jesus in a category all of his own. He is unique, unchallengeable and glorious. Such an appreciation casts a new light on all that we experience. The apostles rejoiced that they were given the privilege to suffer for Jesus. Everything in the Christian life depends upon how we regard Jesus. This reaction has been seen in believers down through the years. When we read of the suffering of modern saints in communist lands, we wonder how they could endure it. Would I be able to do so? Looking at it from the comfort of the western world it seems we would never cope. But if our view of Jesus is high, if we see him as Prince and Saviour, then we would be given the grace to suffer. It is not about strength of character but clarity of spiritual vision.

Opposing Jesus

All men and women are sinners and as such hate authority. From his earliest days a child will kick against the authority of parents. Then when he grows older and becomes aware of the greatest authority possible, namely the authority of God, he will rebel against that. This rebellion is not learnt, and not the result of upbringing or social influence. These may influence it, but the rebellion against God is something we are born with. There is in us all an overwhelming influence called original sin.

This being true, it is not surprising that men were against Jesus, and when Jesus sent apostles to preach the gospel they too faced opposition. It is still the same today. One reason for this is that the gospel of Jesus always exposes sin and makes people feel guilty. The Sanhedrin felt this accusation of guilt (v. 28). However, despite the fact that they *were* guilty they refused to face up to this.

As we have already mentioned, when confronted with Jesus the response of the world was to kill him (v. 30). But the last word lies with God not man — God raised him from the dead. Now God insists that we see Jesus as Prince and Saviour; not as a martyr, not as a teacher or healer, but in a category all of his own as Prince and Saviour. The title 'Prince' speaks of his majesty and power. The word 'Saviour' speaks of his unique role as the only one who can redeem guilty sinners. The description of Jesus as 'exalted' in verse 31 shows that God has set the spotlight of heaven's approval to shine on Jesus so that we may see him as he really is. This exaltation is for our sakes so that from the throne of heaven Jesus might give us 'repentance and forgiveness of sin' (v. 31).

To oppose Jesus is madness. It leaves the sinner with no hope and only hell to await him.

Our gospel witness should be so plain that it leaves no room for sinners merely to admire Jesus as a good man. If men and women truly understand what the gospel is saying they will either love it or hate it. John MacArthur asks:

> *If the gospel we preach is not convicting enough to make some men angry, is it convicting enough to bring them to salvation?*

Gamaliel

Gamaliel's counsel to the Sanhedrin in verses 33-39 is sometimes seen as a model of wisdom and balanced thinking, but in fact it is neither. It is the blind leading the blind. Gamaliel was blind as to who Jesus is. He equates him with revolutionaries like Theudas and Judas of Galilee and has no concept of Jesus as Prince and Saviour.

He is also blind in his understanding of the ways of God. His wait-and-see philosophy denied that God had already spoken plainly in raising Jesus from the dead. If men will not accept a risen and exalted Jesus then nothing else will persuade them.

The religious authorities flogged the preachers of the gospel but God richly blessed them (vv. 40-42).

12.
MOVING OUT

Acts 6:1-7

Even in a church so rich in their experience of Christ as the new church at Jerusalem there will be problems. This is because we are in a battle and the devil will never let God's people rest.

The problem arose between two groups in the church: Greek-speaking Jews and Hebrew-speaking Jews. The Greek speakers thought their widows were not getting a fair share of the church's daily food distribution. Such a dispute should never have arisen because there should not be two sorts of Christians in a church whether it is Greek or Hebrew, Jew or Gentile, clever or dull, rich or poor. Once we divide into groups then at some point disputes become inevitable. The wonderful thing about salvation is that we are all one in Christ. This ought not to be a nice theory but a living reality.

The weakness of the church was revealed in that the dispute ever arose at all, but the strength of the church is seen in the way the problem was resolved. It never helps to sweep problems under the carpet or to run away from them. When there is trouble in a church it is only in the church that the matter will be settled.

Don't give up on your church when there are problems. Remember that the greater the blessing the church experiences, so the more likely it is that the devil will stir up trouble. Do not let him win, and take great encouragement from verse 7. Blessings will follow troubles when they are dealt with properly.

Care for the needy

The daily distribution of food to the widows was an expression of the church's care and concern for those among them who were in material need. First-century Jerusalem had no state handouts for the needy and it was left primarily to individuals to help its aged and widowed members. Clearly in the Jerusalem church there was a real sense of 'family' (4:32-37), and their love for each other showed itself in very practical ways. One of these ways was the daily distribution of food for widows.

Such a ministry in a growing church would take some organizing and it appears that the organization was not as good as the intention. The church's motives were good but implementing the motives ran them into trouble. It often does. The devil will see to that as he clearly did in the case at Jerusalem. Whether the complaint of the Greek speakers was justified or not, it had to be dealt with. Problems are never solved by ignoring them and hoping they will go away. In church life problems have to be faced openly so that all can see that the issue is not being ignored.

Christian love has to be more than mere words and fine sentiments. A rich believer was leading his family devotions and praying fervently that the Lord would meet various different needs in the church. After the prayer his son said to him, 'Dad, if I had your cheque book I could answer most of your prayers.'

The solution

'The twelve gathered all the disciples together' or, in other words, they called a church meeting. They clearly had full confidence in the church to solve the problem. Some may have wanted the apostles to take care of the distribution. They were held in high esteem and their decision would have silenced all complaints, but if they did that they would have to neglect the ministry of the Word of God. So this was rejected and instead the church was asked to choose seven men to organize the distribution. These men were not just to be good organizers but men of a high spiritual calibre — 'full of the Spirit and wisdom'.

In some churches today the pastor is expected to do everything. In theory we do not believe in the one-man ministry but in practice we are quite happy to see it function. But no one man can do it all. The ministry of the Word and prayer is a full-time job in and of itself.

Warren Wiersbe says,

> *The apostles studied the situation and concluded that* they *were to blame: they were so busy serving tables that they were neglecting prayer and the ministry of the Word of God. They had created their own problem because they were trying to do too much. Even today,*

some pastors are so busy with secondary tasks that they fail to spend adequate time in study and in prayer. This creates a 'spiritual deficiency' in the church that makes it easy for problems to develop.

Have you ever thought how you could help take some of the pressure off your pastor? Perhaps if you volunteered to do some sick visiting it would help. Don't think you are too young to do this. Many older folk who are shut-in would love to have a visit from a youngster.

Deacons

The word 'deacon' is not used to describe the men chosen, but they were called to serve the church and that is what a deacon does. Their work is not inferior to those who preach because both are needed in the church if it is to function properly. Both ministries need spiritual men to fulfil them. The tasks were different and separate, but both worked to the end of serving the church and glorifying God. The deacon came into being to set the preachers free from everything except prayer and ministry.

John Stott says,

A vital principle is illustrated in this incident, which is of urgent importance to the church today. It is that God calls all his people to ministry, that he calls different people to different ministries, and that those called to 'prayer and the ministry of the word' must on no account allow themselves to be distracted from their priorities.

The problem arose because of rapid growth in the church and it could have resulted in a split fellowship. Instead it was dealt with urgently and properly and the end result was even more rapid growth (v. 7).

13.

MOVING OUT

Acts 6:8 – 7:60

One of the seven chosen was Stephen and his ministry soon broadened beyond serving tables to the ministry of the word. This brought him into a bitter conflict with the Jewish religious leaders, which led to false accusations being laid against him to stop him preaching. Stephen's answer to these accusations in chapter seven is a brilliant review of God's dealing with Israel from the time of Abraham, and culminates in the strong accusation of verses 51-53.

The speech

Warren Wiersbe sums up the speech as follows:

> *This is the longest address in the Book of Acts and one of the most important. In it, Stephen reviewed the history of Israel and the contributions made by their revered leaders: Abraham (vv. 2-8), Joseph (vv. 9-17), Moses (vv. 18-44), Joshua (vv. 45), and David and Solomon (vv. 46-50). But this address was more than a recitation of familiar facts; it was also a refutation of their indictments against Stephen and a revelation of their own national*

sins. Stephen proved from their own Scriptures that the Jewish nation was guilty of worse sins than those they had accused him of committing. What were these sins?

They misunderstood their own spiritual roots (vv. 1-8).
They rejected their God-sent deliverers (7:9-36).
They disobeyed their law (7:37-43).
They despised their temple (vv. 44-50).
They stubbornly resisted their God and his truth (7:51-53).

Death

The result was that Stephen became the first Christian to die for his faith in Christ. Sadly, since then many believers have gone down the road to martyrdom, but we can say with confidence that anyone who dies for Christ does not die alone. Christ will be with him in a special way.

The triune God in all his majesty was with Stephen. Filled with the Holy Spirit, Stephen saw Jesus on the right hand of God (v. 55). He saw something in his death that he had never seen in his life. Not only did he see Jesus but also something of the spirit of Jesus became his. Compare verse 60 with the words of Jesus at his death, 'Father, forgive them, for they do not know what they are doing' (Luke 23:34).

For a Christian there are worse things than dying. Unfaithfulness to our Saviour is far worse, as is every sin that dishonours his name. To die well is to die faithful to Christ, knowing the comfort of his presence in death and the assurance of resurrection to eternal life. Death is not some terrifying unknown for the Christian. We know more about what will happen to us when we die than we do about what will happen to us next year. The Bible says we will be with the Lord and we shall be like him. We shall awake to a new day. Matthew Henry said that it will be like putting our clothes off to be mended and pressed ready for the great coronation day.

Dying may be difficult for the Christian, with the pain and anguish that may be involved, but death itself should pose no problem. People without Christ are terrified by death, and quite rightly so, because after death there is the judgement. Vavasor Powell, the Welsh Puritan, said, 'The fear of death is engrafted in the common nature of all men, but faith works it out of Christians.' This should be the experience of all believers, but, sadly, it is not always true, and we allow the world's attitude towards death to affect us.

It is not unusual that when a Christian is dying the family takes every precaution to keep the truth from him. Why is this? Is death for us so final and awful? If the family is not Christian and the person who is dying is not a Christian, then we can understand this attitude and the reasoning behind it. One might even go so far as to say that on a rare occasion, in certain circumstances, withholding the truth from a Christian may be wise, but surely not generally. Such a position makes ministering to the dying saint impossible, because everyone is acting a part, and the truth is being suppressed.

What a Christian needs, above all when he is dying, is to know the love and peace of God. To have the things of God ministered to him is his right and privilege. He must be reminded that death has lost its sting and the grave its victory; he must be shown again that the victory of Christ on his behalf is better than any medication.

The spirit, saved and washed in the blood of Jesus, goes immediately to heaven. Jesus said, 'Today you will be with me in Paradise,' and that is why Paul could say with every confidence that 'to die is gain'. In 2 Corinthians 5:8, the apostle tells us that to be away from the body is to be home with the Lord.

The body goes to the grave, to decay and corruption, to await the coming of the Lord and the resurrection. The promise of Jesus is that he will raise us up on the last day (see John 6:39,40,44,54; and 1 Corinthians 15:42-44,51-57). At the resurrection the body and spirit will be united to be for ever with the Lord.

14.
MOVING OUT

Acts 8:1-25

We are introduced for the first time to Saul of Tarsus. His opposition to Christianity was total — he approved of the stoning of Stephen and was determined to destroy the church. It would seem impossible that such a man could ever be converted, but he was. God's grace is stronger than man's hatred. If grace could have been resisted Saul would probably have achieved it, but saving grace overcomes all opposition. Grace has to be irresistible or none of us would be saved.

Philip's ministry in Samaria was attended with remarkable blessing, so much so that a local man of some reputation was fascinated by all that was going on.

Simon the Sorcerer

Without question the greatest delusion anyone can have is to think that he is saved when in fact he is not. Simon the Sorcerer, referred to here in Acts 8, fooled himself with this delusion and for a while the church also was deceived.

Simon was one of the most prominent men in Samaria. Clearly he had an exalted opinion about himself: 'He boasted that he was someone great' (v. 9). The people agreed with him and thought of him as some kind of deity. They were impressed with his ability to perform magic and sorcery. What exactly this was we do not know, but it was impressive. Simon's self-esteem and public status depended upon this ability, so when Philip came to Samaria preaching and performing signs and wonders, Simon's standing in the community was threatened.

He was now not the only one with remarkable powers and it appeared that Philip's power was greater than Simon's, so Simon 'followed Philip everywhere, astonished by the great signs and miracles he saw' (v. 13). Simon the Sorcerer was so impressed that he professed salvation and was baptized. The Christians probably considered this an exciting event. Here was one of the most powerful men in the city professing salvation and becoming a Christian. But it is clear from Acts 8 that Simon's attraction to Christianity was not caused by any conviction of personal sin, but by the professional interest of a magician in the abilities of someone whom he considered to be a rival.

Simon, we are told, believed and was baptized. These are both activities the New Testament urges upon sinners; but what did Simon believe? Did he believe he was a sinner under the wrath and judgement of the holy God? Did he see that his old life of self-esteem and magic was wholly wrong and that he needed to repent of it? Baptism cannot take away sin and therefore it cannot save. It is merely an outward sign of an inward work of grace that has already taken place. Sadly, it became apparent that Simon knew nothing of grace, for his 'heart [was] not right before God' (v. 21) and he was still 'captive to sin' (v. 23).

There are many in our churches who, like Simon, have made an outward profession of faith but lack the essential inward work of grace that alone saves. Such people can fool both themselves and the church; but they do not fool God.

Exposed

Simon's true spiritual condition was revealed when Peter and John came to Samaria. They prayed for the new converts and laid hands on them, and when they did so the Samaritan Christians received the Holy Spirit. Simon was greatly excited by this and wanted this power to add to his own repertoire of magic tricks, so he offered Peter and John money if they would tell him how it was done.

Peter's response was devastating as in a few sentences he exposed Simon as the sorcerer who still had no concept of salvation: 'May your money perish with you...! You have no part or share in this ministry, because your heart is not right before God' (v. 20). Simon, for all his profession and baptism, knew nothing of God. He thought of God in the same way as he thought of his magic abilities. He did not understand that nothing God has is for sale. If a man thinks he can buy salvation, or perhaps earn it by his own efforts, he is revealing a total ignorance as to the holiness of God and the depths of his own sin.

Simon's problem was that he was still completely absorbed in signs and wonders. He saw them as a means to continue being somebody special. In fact he had no desire to change what he was, only to establish his old position more firmly. He was not concerned about salvation, only about self-esteem and position. For him, signs and wonders were a means to that end.

True salvation

Peter showed Simon what was wrong with him spiritually and what he needed to do in order to become a Christian.

The first thing that Peter told him was: 'Your heart is not right before God' (v. 21). This was true of Simon, and it is true of everyone who has not repented of their sin and trusted in Christ alone for salvation.

Secondly, Peter told Simon, 'Repent of this wickedness' (v. 22). Repentance is not a case of trying your best to put right all the sin there is in your life. Repentance means that the sinner, conscious of his guilt, and aware of the mercy of God in Christ, turns from his sin to God. The repentant sinner knows a loathing and a hatred of sin and a great desire to live in obedience to God. He will cry to God for mercy and pardon.

Finally, Peter urged Simon, '...pray to the Lord. Perhaps he will forgive you' (v. 22). The prayer for forgiveness of sin is not a polite petition but a cry of desperation. Salvation becomes the most important thing in one's life. An urgency is created in our hearts by the Holy Spirit that will know no relief until salvation comes. It is the Lord alone who can forgive sin, so it is to him alone that the repentant sinner goes.

Whether Simon did this or not we are not told, but the New Testament does tell us that when we come to Christ in repentance and faith, he will receive us and forgive us all our sin. This is true salvation. It is not a fascination with miracles or anything else, but a soul made right with God through the merit and grace of the Lord Jesus Christ.

15.

MOVING OUT

Acts 8:26-40

God's amazing love for individuals is seen in the story of Philip and the Ethiopian. The Lord took Philip from the rich blessings of Samaria where crowds were being saved to the middle of a desert to preach the gospel to one man.

The Ethiopian was clearly seeking God and had gone to Jerusalem to worship (v. 27). He was returning home having obtained a copy of the prophecy of Isaiah and was reading what we know as chapter 53. Clear though Isaiah 53 is to any Christian, to a non-Christian it is totally confusing and needs explaining (vv. 30-31). There are many today that flatly refuse to believe that this chapter is talking about Jesus, but Philip had no doubt (v. 35). And by the time he had finished preaching the Ethiopian had no doubt either (vv. 36-39).

This man's heart was open for God to speak to him and God spoke through the Scriptures and through a preacher. Sinners need to hear about Jesus and particularly what he did for them on the cross. This is the message that sets them free from the grip of sin.

The gospel's message is that when Jesus died on the cross he did so in the place of guilty sinners to save them from God's anger against their sin and the judgement they deserve. Jesus alone was innocent of sin and therefore he alone could act as our substitute. He stood in the place of his people and took the punishment they deserved.

The cross was God's supreme act of love and grace. The Ethiopian believed this and was saved. No wonder then that he 'went on his way rejoicing' (v. 39).

Today

Does God still go to such remarkable lengths to save individuals today? Of course he does. God never saves en masse. Even at Pentecost when 3,000 were saved they were all saved one at a time. Conversion is very personal and God deals with us as individuals. Most of us are saved by the preaching of the gospel but God has to go to extraordinary lengths sometimes to get us to hear the gospel. The following testimony is proof of this.

> *One Sunday afternoon I had a strange and strong urge to go to church that evening. This desire was unwarranted and I could not understand it, but the urge was irresistible. So that night, without any mention to Mary, I went back to the same church.*
>
> *I parked the car well away from the church and sneaked in at the back, ten minutes before the service was due to commence. I kept asking myself what I was doing there. Surely there was not really a God — Jesus cannot truthfully be real.*
>
> *I picked up a hymn-book and as I thumbed through it I noticed an extra hymn, 'Amazing Grace', inserted inside the back cover. The hymns in that particular*

church were not announced in advance. I had an idea. I would test God. I bowed my head and prayed that if God really did exist, then that night we would sing that particular hymn. A man then entered the church wearing an American sweatshirt with the number 47 on the front and back — so I prayed again, adding hymn number 47 to my device to test God.

Eventually the service began and the minister announced the first hymn — 'Amazing Grace'. Though initially shaken, I put this down to coincidence, but when after the opening prayer we sang hymn number 47, I wondered what was happening. Could there really be a God? The minister then began to preach the gospel, and suddenly I came under a tremendous conviction of sin. It felt like a volcano within me. I knew for the first time that God really did exist, and also that he judged.

The gospel did not finish there. God not only revealed to me my sins but he also led me to Jesus. How that volcano erupted inside me! I could not restrain myself any longer and I remember so well the tears of shame and the tears of joy as I was visited and dealt with by God. The joy, the happiness — I had met with Jesus and I left that church a new man.[1]

Note

1. Extract taken from *I will never become a Christian*, Peter Jeffery, pp.60-1.

16.
MOVING OUT

Acts 9:1-19

In Saul of Tarsus we see a man vigorously opposed to Jesus (v. 1). He hated the Lord and all who followed him. In his mind and conscience he was not opposed to God, only to Jesus. But a man opposed to Jesus cannot be right with God and Saul was soon to discover this.

In the previous chapter we saw a man seeking God; now we see a man who thinks he is doing God's will by persecuting Christians. The Ethiopian had just discovered the writings of Isaiah; Saul had known them all his life. The Ethiopian was persuaded that Isaiah 53 was talking of Jesus. Saul would have passionately denied that. Here were two very different men; but God saved them both. The breadth of divine grace is staggering. We could expect the Ethiopian to be saved eventually, but who would have expected a man like Saul of Tarsus to come to Christ?

It may be there are people of your acquaintance like Saul and you can see no hope of them ever becoming a Christian. Take heart from the power of saving grace. It is no more difficult for God to save a Saul than an Ethiopian. But the Sauls of this world have to be humbled by God. How hard it must have been for Saul the Pharisee, the deeply religious man, to have to admit that he was really a stranger to God and all along had been wrong about Jesus.

Do not be embarrassed to speak to your Saul-like friends about Jesus. It may be a red rag to a bull but it is the only thing that will save them.

The actions of Saul in verses 1-2 appear to be those of a strong, determined man who knew exactly what he believed. But in fact they were totally unreasonable. To take his murderous threats to Damascus was the action of a fanatic not a strong man. God was pointing Saul in one direction and he was rebelling and going the opposite way. That is why Jesus said to him, 'It is hard for you to kick against the goads' (Acts 26:14). His persecutions were clearly difficult for the church but they were also hard on Saul himself. It is always hard for a sinner to fight against the grace of God. God will always win even when the opposition is as formidable as Saul of Tarsus.

Saul's conversion was so crucial for the spread of Christianity that the events that occurred on the Damascus road are told three times in Acts. You may not feel that your conversion was as dramatic as Saul's but all conversions are basically the same. For any sinner to come to Christ he must have the following four things.

1. His mind informed — as to who he is dealing with. In verse 5 Saul is confronted with the living Christ. The one he had written off as a fraud was demonstrated beyond all doubt to be the Son of God. No one can be a Christian without a personal encounter with Jesus. Our experience in conversion will vary one from another but all need to realize that our unbelief is an opposition to the living Jesus.

2. His conscience aroused. Saul's actions were rebellion in the guise of service. He had been opposing God. It may be that his conscience had been stirred as he listened to

Stephen, but he smothered this. He was fighting against admitting that he was a sinner and that Jesus was the only Saviour. Many are like that and need Jesus to arouse their conscience to see and feel their true spiritual condition.

3. *His emotions stirred.* Saul was 'trembling and astonished' (v. 6, NKJV). All his apparent self-confidence vanished in the presence of Jesus. The man would have had to be a statue if his emotions were not stirred. He trembled in fear of the consequence of his sins and is astonished that though he was sincere he had been terribly wrong. Charles Spurgeon said, 'A sinner has a heart as well as a head; a sinner has emotions as well as thoughts, and we must appeal to both. A sinner will never be converted until his emotions are stirred.'

4. *His will surrendered.* The question of verse 6 (NKJV), 'Lord, what do you want me to do?', is crucial to salvation. Here is a soul realizing that all he has done is wrong, so he must now do what Jesus wants. Jesus wants us to repent and believe in him. There is no salvation without repentance and no repentance without conviction of sin. But when these are truly present there will be a humble surrender of the will to Christ.

The newborn soul is not left to its own devices. God brings an experienced Christian named Ananias alongside Saul to encourage and instruct him. It may be that you could be a help to some new convert. If so, don't smother him with too much fuss. Just be there when he needs help. Point him to the right books to read. Show him around the Bible until he is familiar with God's Word. Pray with him and encourage him to become involved in the life of the church.

17.

MOVING OUT

Acts 9:20-43

Saul's conversion was so amazing that people could not believe it (v. 21). Even the Christians had a hard time believing he was saved (v. 26). Thank God for Barnabas who could see what God had done and paved the way for Saul to be accepted by the believers.

We are not to be naive and accept every profession of faith as genuine, but neither are we to limit the power of God. There have sadly been many professions of faith in every church which did not last very long, but this is not to make us sceptical when we hear of conversions. A true convert will reveal the validity of his experience by his love and passion for Christ (v. 28) and by his Christlike spirit (v. 36). Dorcas would never have had the influence upon the world that Saul was to have but she certainly made a great impression upon those who knew her (v. 39). Dorcas could not speak boldly in public about Jesus but in private her actions spoke volumes.

Every church needs its Sauls and Dorcases — the public speakers and the quiet workers. The church at Joppa was richly blessed by Dorcas being there. This woman is a great example to us all. There is so much work that needs doing that the great Saul could never do. It takes a Dorcas to knit and sew. Saul could make tents but could he make a sweater?

Your church needs the gifts you have — whatever they may be. Don't covet the prominent position but aim that when you die you will leave behind a sweet savour of Christ in the hearts of your friends.

The contrast between the ministry of Saul and that of Dorcas could not be more striking. Most young Christians would probably like to be a Saul and take on the world for Christ. Compared to this the ministry of Dorcas was very ordinary and totally lacking in excitement. But the fact is that for every great preacher there are a thousand like Dorcas who quietly get on with the work of the local church.

What we are doing in the church will only be effective if we are doing what God wants us to do. In God's sight 'doing good and helping the poor' is as much to his glory as 'speaking boldly in the name of the Lord'.

Do you covet a ministry which the Lord has not equipped you for? Many a young believer has trained for the ministry or gone to the mission field convinced this was God's will for his life. But subsequent events proved they were wrong. Their gifts and temperament made these tasks impossible for them and years of struggle and disillusionment follow.

John MacArthur tells the following story:

> *Many years ago five young college students made their way to London to hear Charles Haddon Spurgeon preach. Arriving early at the Metropolitan Tabernacle, they found the doors still locked. While they waited on the steps, a man approached them. 'Would you like to see the heating apparatus of this church?' he asked. That was*

> *not what they had come for, but they agreed to go with him. He led them into the building, down a long flight of stairs, and into a hallway. At the end of the hallway he opened a door into a large room filled with seven hundred people on their knees praying. 'That', said their guide (who was none other than Spurgeon himself), 'is the heating apparatus of this church.'*

You may never preach from the pulpit of your church but you should always be in the prayer meeting, if at all possible.

18.

MOVING OUT

Acts 10:1-22

If ever a man could be saved by his own actions it was Cornelius. Look at the description of these actions in verse 2. Here was a remarkable man — genuine, sincere, devout and earnest. But he was still an unenlightened soul groping after God.

God is impressed with Cornelius (v. 4). He is a man living according to the light and understanding he has, but God does not leave him there. Cornelius needs to hear the gospel so he is told to send for Simon Peter (v. 5). The reason for sending for Peter is made clear in 11:14. It is not Cornelius's good works that will save him but the gospel Peter will preach to him. In other words, though God approves of this Roman's goodness he still treats him as a sinner who needs to be saved.

God sends an angel to Cornelius, not to preach the gospel to him, but to tell him to send for a man who will tell him the good news of what God has done for sinners. Men, not angels, are given the responsibility of evangelism. What a privilege this is for all Christians!

If Cornelius could not be saved by his own goodness, this should once and for all shut the door on hope of any man or woman being saved by their own actions. Sinners need the gospel and it is our God-given responsibility to tell it to them. It may be that God has you in mind particularly to speak to a Cornelius of your acquaintance. Praise God for the privilege and ask him to use you in this person's salvation.

Peter's vision

Clearly it was God's will that Peter should preach to Cornelius, but in normal circumstances Peter would never have done so. Peter, like most Jews, had a deep inbred prejudice against Gentiles. It is this prejudice that the vision is intended to shatter.

The Jews thought that God was only interested in them and found it difficult to understand that people of other nationalities could also benefit from the grace of God. Remember that these were men filled with the Holy Spirit. They had been used mightily by God. Yet because of this prejudice they had no great desire to spread the gospel to other nations. We all need to seek the fulness of the Spirit, and long for more of the Spirit's power in our lives, but let us not be so foolish as to think that this will make all our weaknesses and problems disappear. That was not the case in New Testament times and never has been since.

Even a man filled with the Holy Spirit can be wrong unless he heeds the Word of God. If these men had listened to Jesus when he told them to go to all nations they would have seen that the gospel was for everyone. But their actions were affected by their prejudices and this threatened to hinder the work of evangelism.

The Jewish prejudice was so deep-rooted in the thinking of God's people that in order to remove it he had to do two remarkable things. First of all, he gave a special vision to Peter (see Acts 10:1-23) to persuade him to go and preach to the Roman, Cornelius. Peter's prejudice is clearly spelt out in Acts 10:28, and it is evident from Acts 11:2-3 that this attitude was shared by many of his fellow believers. Using Peter's account of the conversion of the Gentiles, God dealt firmly with these wrong attitudes, so that eventually the whole church was constrained to confess, 'So then, God has granted even the Gentiles repentance unto life' (Acts 11:18). This was a remarkable breakthrough, leading to a new understanding of the breadth of divine love and grace. However, to understand something is not the same as to practise it.

The second thing God did, therefore, was to make sure that they spread the gospel abroad by using persecution to get them out of Jerusalem (Acts 11:19). Even then, as we read at the end of verse 19, they at first preached the message of Christ only to Jews. They seemed blind to the glaring inconsistency between their declaration in verse 18 and their limited vision in verse 19. The difference between these two verses is the difference between what we acknowledge to be true and what we actually do. We can apply this principle to many aspects of our Christian life, but let us confine ourselves here to the context of evangelism. It is not enough to have a theoretical belief in the evangelization of the world. We must actually get on with the work in our own backyard! Surely no Bible-believing Christian can doubt that when Jesus told the first believers to be his witnesses, he was speaking as much to us as to them. Every Christian in every generation is to be a witness for the Lord Jesus Christ.

19.

MOVING OUT

Acts 10:23-48

Before we examine Peter's message we need to consider the attitude of Cornelius as he heard the gospel: 'It was good of you to come. Now we are all here in the presence of God to listen to everything the Lord has commanded you to tell us.'

There was a real sense of the privilege of being allowed to hear God's Word and eagerness and desire to listen. He acknowledged that the message was not from Peter but from God.

Here was no clock-watcher wondering when the preacher was going to finish. Here was no pew critic taking the sermon to pieces. Cornelius was aware that God was speaking and he was eager to hear every word. Is that how you listen to the preaching of the Word of God?

What was it that Peter told the centurion that led to his conversion? He was told of the grace of God (vv. 34-35) — God shows no favouritism. The gospel is for all types of people and all nationalities. There is no one beyond the grace of God. It can reach the most unlikely people and this ought to give us confidence in proclaiming it. The message itself said basically three things about Jesus.

- *His life* (vv. 36-38). Jesus is no ordinary man. He is Lord of all. There is no one like Jesus and his love and power are limitless.

- *His death* (v. 39). The gracious Jesus was killed by being hung on a tree. He was crucified. Men firmly and viciously rejected him.

- *His resurrection* (v. 40). In spite of all the evil that men did, God had the last word and raised Jesus from the dead. Men cannot get rid of Jesus because he is Lord of all.

As Peter was preaching, the power of the Holy Spirit was felt (v. 44). Conviction and repentance were given to Cornelius and to all those present. This combination of faithful preaching and the power of the Holy Spirit are always the irresistible tools God uses to save souls. We should pray that we see more of this today.

In the light of the description of Cornelius in verse 2, we have to ask what was the sin he needed to confess. The truth is that we do not know; but he knew and God knew. Cornelius knew he was a sinner and longed for pardon and salvation. He heard the gospel, believed it, repented and came in faith to Jesus. There is no bypassing the gospel, the Holy Spirit, conviction of sin and repentance if sinners are to be saved. Easy, comfortable-sounding sermons may be attractive to people, but what saves is the personal conviction of the harsh reality of sin in all its ugliness. Sinners need to be told that they are unacceptable to God and that Jesus alone is the way of salvation.

The purpose of the gospel is to bring rebel sinners to God, and make them his children and heirs. Through the gospel they are born anew, forgiven, reconciled, accepted and adopted, all in Christ. Though some trust in morality and good works, and others in philosophy and religion, the fact is that only Jesus Christ can make us accepted by a holy God. It is crucial that we are clear about this in our thinking. The Word of God says that Jesus Christ is the only way to God. That is the uniform teaching of Scripture, as exemplified by Jesus (John 14:6), Peter (Acts 4:12) and Paul (1 Timothy 2:5). It is not being broad-minded and tolerant to say that all religions are the same and that all roads lead to God. To say that is to call Jesus a liar, for his claims are exclusive. The New Testament will not allow us to think otherwise and God will not condone such teaching. The evangelism of the early church clearly told sinners that 'There is no other name under heaven given to men by which we must be saved' (Acts 4:12).

We shall not be surprised, therefore, to learn that the message of New Testament evangelism is Christ himself. If we could ask Paul what he preached, he would reply that he preached 'Jesus Christ and him crucified' (1 Corinthians 2:2). God had chosen him to 'preach him [Christ] among the Gentiles' (Galatians 1:16), and the apostle considered it an enormous privilege to preach 'the unsearchable riches of Christ' (Ephesians 3:8). What is it, then, to 'preach Christ'? It is to proclaim who he is and what he has done.

20.
MOVING OUT

Acts 11:1-30

Chapter eleven is virtually a repetition of chapter ten, as Peter recounts the events to the church at Jerusalem. The believers had greeted the news of the conversion of Cornelius with criticism, not praise. This Jewish anti-Gentile prejudice was strong even in regenerate men and women.

We all bring pre-conversion baggage with us when we are saved and we have to be careful that this is not allowed to hinder the work of the gospel. Examine your life to see if you have any of this baggage still with you. Sometimes it is not easy to recognize. For older folk it may be traditional ways and things that are dear to them. For youngsters it may be taste in music, but all must be subjected to the will of God and what God is doing for the good of the church and the salvation of lost souls. It would be convenient if the Scriptures spelt out in detail the right and wrong way on such matters, but they do not. Nevertheless, biblical principles can show us what God requires of us.

When the church at Jerusalem heard what God had done for Cornelius their prejudices were silenced and they praised God. Unfortunately this did not appear to have much practical effect and when some of them went to Antioch they still preached only to Jews (v. 19).

Telling the good news

In Acts 11:19-20 the evangelism of the early church is very simply described as telling the people 'the good news about the Lord Jesus'. They preached, proclaimed, heralded, declared, or stated the truth about Jesus. There was no hesitation, nor was the message watered down. Their evangelism was not half-hearted or reluctant. They believed that without Jesus people would go to hell, and this added a note of urgency to their message. But they also believed that before time began God, in love and mercy, had purposed to save a great multitude that no man could number. This added a note of joy and confidence to their message.

The early church was a telling church. Why was this? Were not music and drama available as means of communication in the society of their day? Yes, but telling or preaching was God's way of communicating the gospel, and it still is. The principle presented in Romans 10:14-15 is still relevant: how can they believe unless they hear, and how can they hear without someone preaching to them?

Somehow we have come to believe that telling or preaching the good news about Jesus is the work of the minister from the pulpit, while personal evangelism consists primarily in sharing our testimony with unbelievers. It must be good for Christians to give their testimony to non-Christians, but unless that testimony is accompanied by a clear, even if simple, declaration of who Jesus is and what he has done for sinners, then the testimony will have the wrong effect. It will make men look at us, rather than to Christ, or else our story will be dismissed as some mystical experience: 'That's fine for you, but not relevant for me.' It is the truth about Jesus that puts men and women 'on the spot' and forces them to think seriously about themselves and God. Even though all Christians cannot be preachers from the pulpit, we are all meant to tell the good news about the Lord Jesus.

The Lord's hand

Biblical truth is indispensable to evangelism but it is not in itself enough. The aim of the gospel is not only to teach sinners the truth; pre-eminently it is to save them, and something else is needed if sinners are to believe and be saved. We are told in Acts 11:21 that at Antioch 'a great number of people believed', and there were two causes of this. There was the faithful witness of the Christians and there was the power of God using that witness to convict and convert sinners. William Arnot, a Scottish preacher of the nineteenth century, wrote:

> *The instrument is all human, but the power is all Divine. We learn here with great simplicity and clarity these two things: (1) that in conversion the hand of the Lord operates; but (2) that it operates through the ministry of men. In this work men can do nothing without God; but in this work God will do nothing without men.*

It is not that God cannot do anything without men but that he chooses to use men in the work of salvation. Paul sets out the basic principle in 1 Corinthians 3:5-9. He describes himself and other preachers as 'servants, through whom you came to believe'. One servant planted the seed, another watered it, 'but God made it grow'. In the work of evangelism, Christians have the amazing privilege of being 'God's fellow workers'. We see this principle in action in Acts 10 and 11. An angel appeared to Cornelius, not to preach the gospel to him but to tell him to send for Peter: 'He will bring you a message through which you and all your household will be saved' (Acts 11:14). God uses men to evangelize, not angels. But the point is also made in Acts 11:15 that the faithful witness of men, though crucial, is not enough: 'As I began to speak, the Holy Spirit came on them.' Men are taken into partnership with God, but the power belongs to God alone.

21.
MOVING OUT

Acts 12:1-25

Opposition from the world very often follows blessings in the church. This should not surprise us because we see it so often in the New Testament, and here it is again in Acts 12. The apostle James was killed and it looked as though Peter would suffer the same end: 'but the church was earnestly praying to God for him' (v. 5). When the civil powers seem determined to stamp out Christianity there are only two things believers can do. They can either cower with fear and this will ensure that the Herods of this world will triumph, or they can pray and that will ensure that God would be glorified.

God's answer to the prayer was remarkable (vv. 6-11) — so remarkable that even the Christians had a hard time believing it. We do not want to be guilty of the same sort of unbelief as these saints, but we have to be careful and acknowledge that God does not always answer prayer in this way. Shadrach, Meshach and Abednego had the perfect balance in their words to Nebuchadnezzar: 'If we are thrown into the blazing furnace, the God we serve is able to save us from it, and he will rescue us from your hand, O king. But even if he does not, we want you to know, O king, that we will not serve your gods or worship the image of gold you have set up' (Daniel 3:17-18).

God can and does deliver his people in remarkable ways, but even if he does not our faith in him is not to languish in the slightest.

Expectations

This raises the question of what we expect to happen when we pray. Prayer is not about us persuading a reluctant God to do what we think is right. Nor does the power of prayer depend on how many Christians we can get to pray. If one saint or a million pray for something that is outside the will of God, it will avail nothing. Perhaps we spend too much time in prayer asking for things and not enough time dwelling on who God is and seeking to know his purposes. To quote Tozer:

> *In all our praying, however, it is important that we keep in mind that God will not alter his eternal purposes at the word of a man. We do not pray in order to persuade God to change his mind. Prayer is not an assault upon the reluctance of God, nor an effort to secure a suspension of his will for us or for those for whom we pray. Prayer is not intended to overcome God and 'move his arm'. God will never be other than himself, no matter how many people pray, or how long, or how earnestly. What the praying man does is to bring his will into line with the will of God so God can do what he has all along been willing to do. Thus prayer changes the man and enables God to change things in answer to man's prayer.*

This does not mean that we should not plead with God to save souls, but it does mean that we must use prayer to commune with God, to praise him, to delight in him, to worship him and to learn from him what and when he wants things done. This creates a deeper knowledge of God which produces a greater awareness of his power and a greater expectancy in us to see this power at work. It also leads to something of the heart and mind of God being fashioned in us. Then, like our Saviour, we shall weep for souls. Such weeping will not be merely a demonstration of emotion on our part, but a reflection of the sentiments of God. When this takes place we can expect to see divine power saving the lost.

BIBLIOGRAPHY

Arnot, William, *Studies in Acts*, Kregel, 1978.

Bonar, Andrew, *Robert Murray M'Cheyne, Memoirs and remains,* Banner of Truth.

Jeffery, Peter, *I will never become a Christian*, Bryntirion Press.

Lloyd-Jones, Dr D. Martyn, *Authentic Christianity: Studies in the book of Acts,* Crossway, 2000.

MacArthur, John, *Commentary on Acts,* Moody, 1994.

Spurgeon, Charles, *Autobiography: The early years*, Banner of Truth.

Stott, John, *Acts*, IVP, 1990.

Wiersby, Warren, *Be Dynamic*, CVP, 1987.

A wide range of excellent books on spiritual subjects is available from Evangelical Press. Please write to us for your free catalogue or contact us by e-mail.

Evangelical Press
Faverdale North, Darlington, DL3 0PH, England

e-mail: sales@evangelicalpress.org

Evangelical Press USA
P. O. Box 825, Webster, New York 14580, USA

e-mail: usa.sales@evangelicalpress.org

web: http://www.evangelicalpress.org